The Trumpet Co

MW00581767

Transcribed or composed by Bernard Fitzgerald

Contents

*Program notes are in the piano part.

Editor: Thom Proctor
Art: Joann Carrera

2

Scarlatti Suite
Allessandro Scarlatti (1660-1725)

The Scarlatti Suite consists of three movements, Allegro-Adagio-Allegro. Scarlatti was an Italian composer from the area of Naples. He composed operas, solo voice and choral cantatas, oratorios, masses, madrigals and chamber music. He was the father of another famous composer, Domenico. The pieces in this suite come from three Neapolitan songs from his era. This is a level III piece for trumpet.

Scarlatti Suite

I

Allegro

A. SCARLATTI (1660-1725)
Arranged by BERNARD FITZGERALD

EL96106

4

II
Adagio

8

III
Allegro

Allegro guisto (♩ = 126)

12

Aria (Bist du bei mir)
Johann Sebastian Bach (1685-1750)

This piece comes from the Little Notebook for Anna Magdalena Bach. This level II piece for trumpet was originally in the key of E♭ for piano. Anna Magdalena had a decent soprano voice and probably sang this piece, "If Thou Be Near," as she played. Anna Magdalena Bach was Johann's second wife and bore him thirteen children, many of whom were musicians.

Bach Suite
Johann Sebastian Bach (1685-1750)

The four movements in this suite came from three different keyboard works by Bach. The Prelude is from the Short Preludes and Fugues. The Sarabande and the Menuet are from the French Suite No. 1. A sarabande was a slow dance in 3/2 (or in this case 3/4) time and originally came from Spain. The menuet also was a dance in 3/4 time with its origins in France. The final movement, Allegro is from the Partita in b minor. Bach Suite is a level IV in difficulty.

Aria
Bist du bei mir
If Thou be near

J.S. BACH
Arranged by BERNARD FITZGERALD

Moderato

EL96106

Bach Suite
Prelude

J.S. BACH
Transcribed by BERNARD FITZGERALD

18

EL96106

Sarabande

20

EL96106

Menuet

EL96106

Allegro

24

26

EL96106

Introduction and Fantasy
Bernard Fitzgerald (1911-)

This is an original composition written in 1940. It is a one movement piece but with many meter, tempo and style changes. From the dramatic beginning to the lyrical Andante Cantabile section in the middle to the Allegro con brio and Vivo ending, this piece allows the performer ample opportunity for showcasing their abilities. It is of a modern style and definitely a contrast to the baroque-style pieces in this collection.

Sonata VIII
Arcangelo Corelli (1653-1713)

Corelli was a violinist and composer in Rome, Italy. This sonata is taken from his Twelve Solo Sonatas, Opus 5. The four movements are Prelude, Allemande (a moderate tempo dance in 4/4 time), Sarabande, and Gigue (an up-tempo dance in 6/8 or 12/8 time). It is a level III in difficulty.

Allegro
Antonio Vivaldi (1678-1741)

Antonio Vivaldi was a violinist and composer that did most of his composing and performing in Venice, but died in Vienna. He was a prolific composer and wrote 450 concertos for various instruments, his most famous being "The Four Seasons," for violin. He also wrote operas, oratorios, and much church music. Allegro comes from an aria, "Armato face et au quibus," from his oratorio Juditha Triumphans. It is a level IV in difficulty.

Dedicated to my wife

Introduction and Fantasy

B♭ Cornet Solo with Piano Accompaniment

BERNARD FITZGERALD

32

Sonata VIII

ARCANGELO CORELLI
Transcribed by BERNARD FITZGERALD

Prelude

Allemande

Sarabande

Gigue

Allegro
for Trumpet Solo and Piano

ANTONIO VIVALDI
Transcribed by BERNARD FITZGERALD

46

47

EL96106

Aria con Variazioni

George Frederic Handel (1685-1759)

George Frederic Handel was born in Halle, Germany. He first visited England in 1710, and lived much of the rest of his life there, dying in London in 1759. His last six years he lived in total blindness. Aria con Variazioni comes from Handel's Suite No. 5 for harpsichord. The theme is stated in the Andantino section and there follows five variations. The level of difficulty is a V.

Aria con Variazione
(From 5th Harpsichord Suite)

G.F. HANDEL
Transcribed by BERNARD FITZGERALD

EL96106

Var. I

Var. II 6
Poco più mosso

Var. III 8
Un poco meno mosso *slower!*

Var. IV [10]

Poco più mosso

EL96106

Var. V

Allegro molto